I0473534

PURELY PATTERNS

VOL 2

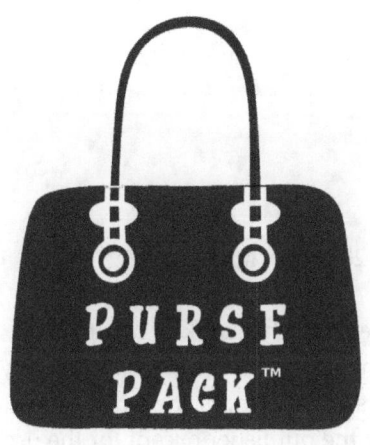

PURSE PACK™

Written and Illustrated by Tina Golden

Copyright © 2019 by Tina Golden

All rights reserved. This book or any portion
thereof may not be reproduced or used in any
manner whatsoever without the express written
permission of the publisher except for the use of
brief quotations in a book review. If images are
used in a review, they must not be of print
quality.

Printed in the United States of America

First Printing, 2019

Tina Golden
Doodletime Design
16 Maple Street
Augusta, ME 04330

www.DoodletimeDesign.com

Thank you for purchasing Purely Patterns Vol.2 Purse Pack™. Each design in this book began as a hand-drawn art piece. The image was then digitized and manipulated using a variety of software to create these lovely detailed coloring pages.

Tips for Coloring

First of all, there is no wrong way to color. Some of the benefits of coloring include lowering anxiety, relieving stress, and inducing a meditative state. These benefits are lost if you feel pressured to color a certain way. That's why these pages are non-representational: they're completely and purposefully non-realistic.

I recommend colored pencils or other dry media for this book, but you can use markers or gel pens if you take some care. Wet media can bleed thru the pages and ruin another design, even with single-sided pages like the ones in this series. To avoid that, make sure to put an extra sheet of paper or cardstock behind the page you're coloring. There are two convenient blotter sheets included at the back of the book that you can tear out for this purpose.

I love seeing how other people color my designs and learning about their techniques, so I'd love to have you share any finished pieces on my Facebook page. And authors and artists thrive on reviews, so please help me out by taking a minute to post a review on Amazon. Your support will enable me to keep bringing you new and exciting coloring books.

See you there!

Tina Golden

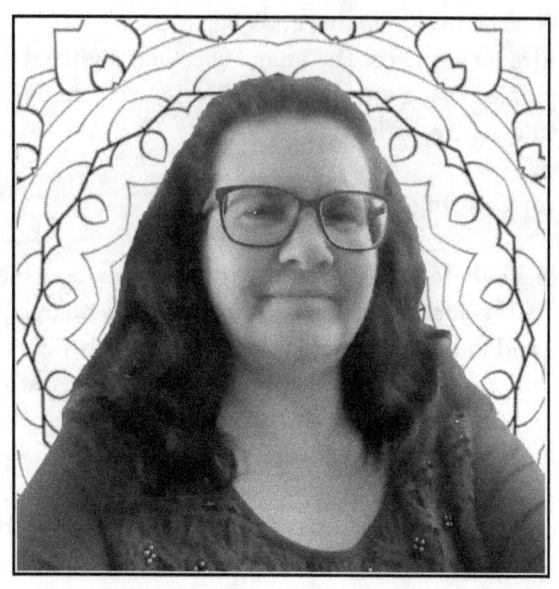

https://www.facebook.com/DoodletimeOriginals

https://www.pinterest.com/doodletimedesign/

https://www.instagram.com/doodletimedesign/

http://DoodletimeDesign.com/YouTube

http://www.amazon.com/author/tinagolden

http://www.DoodletimeDesign.com

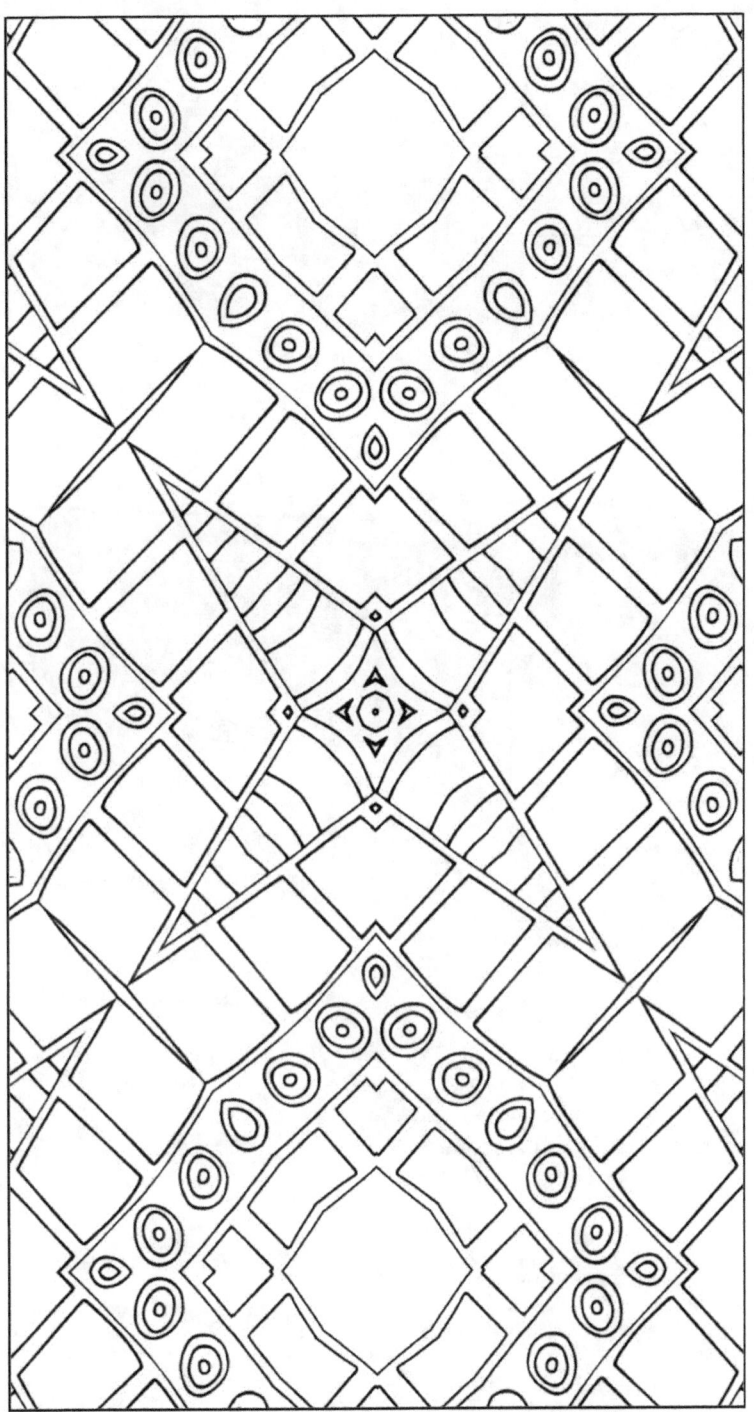

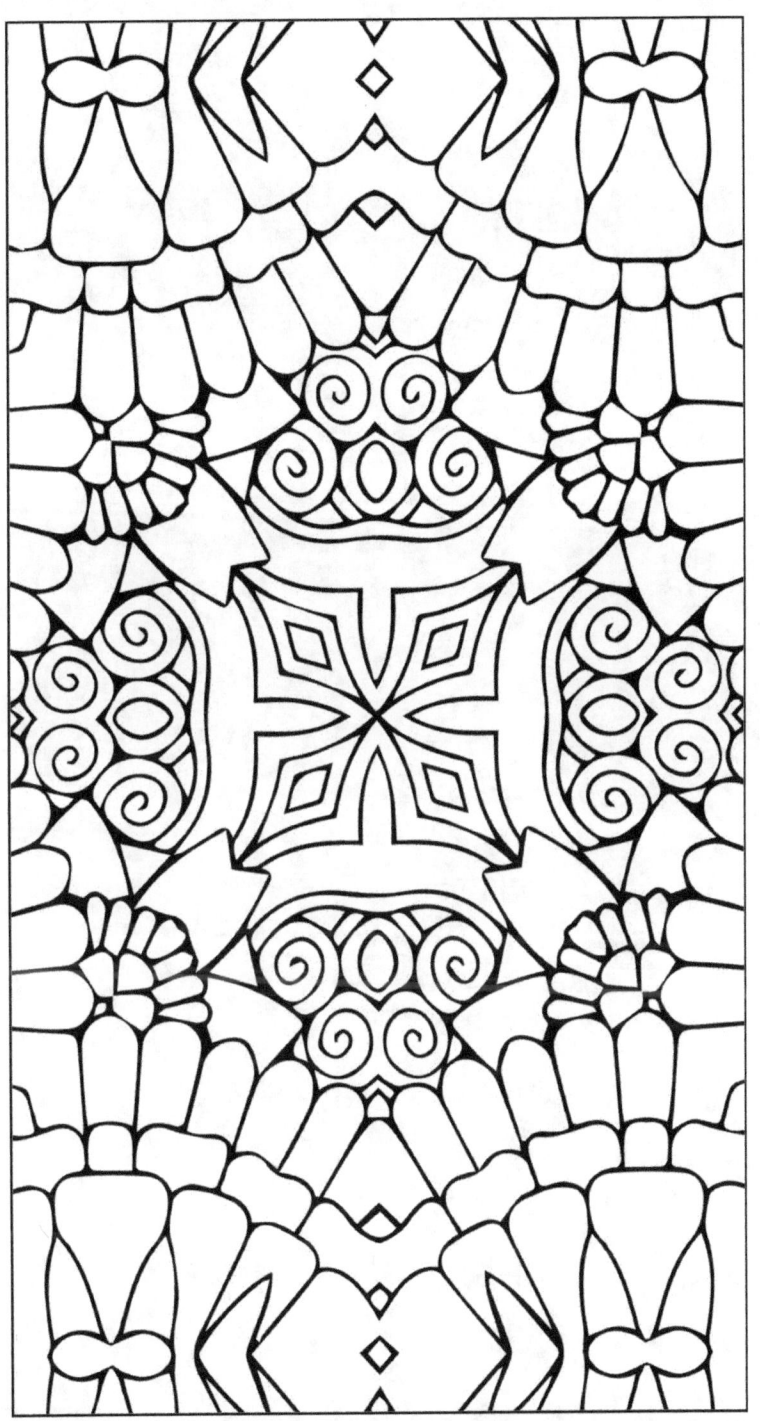

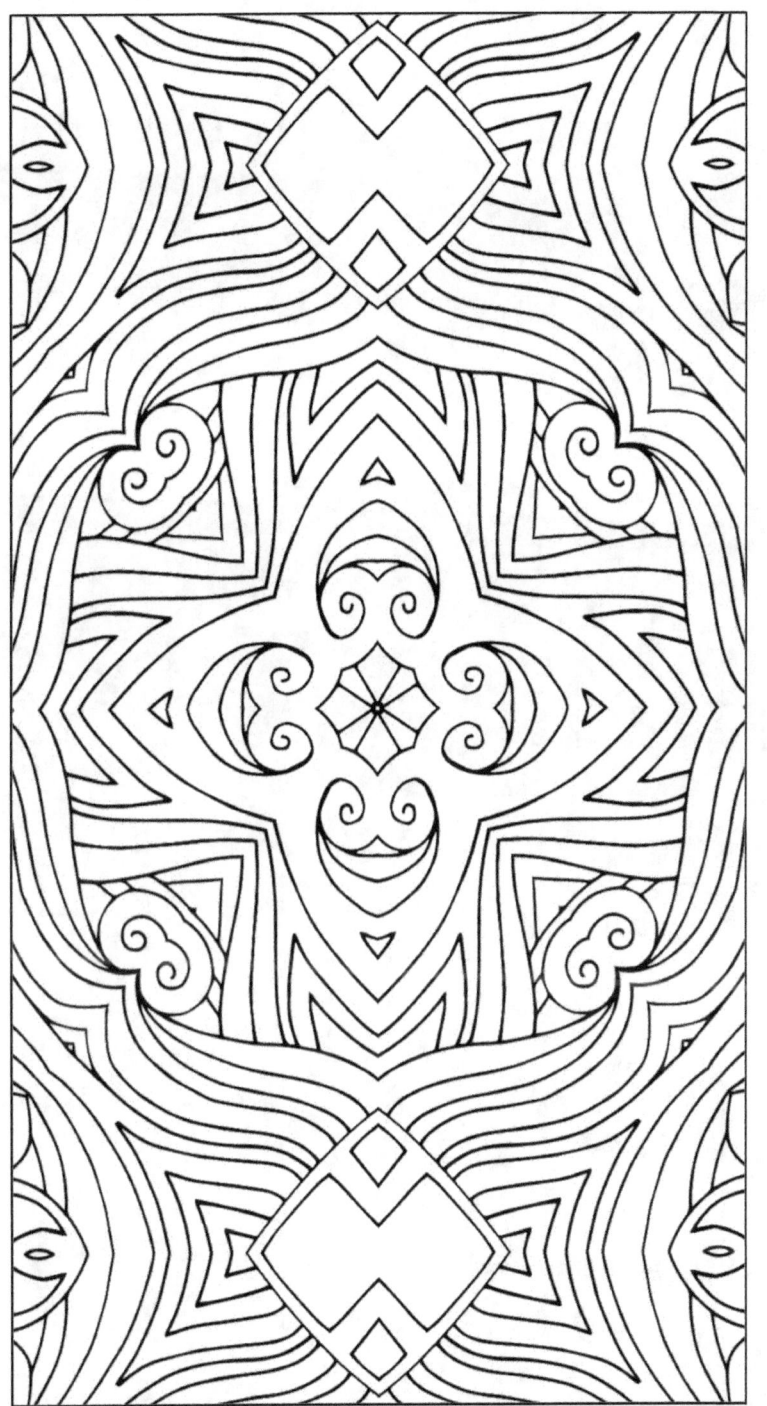

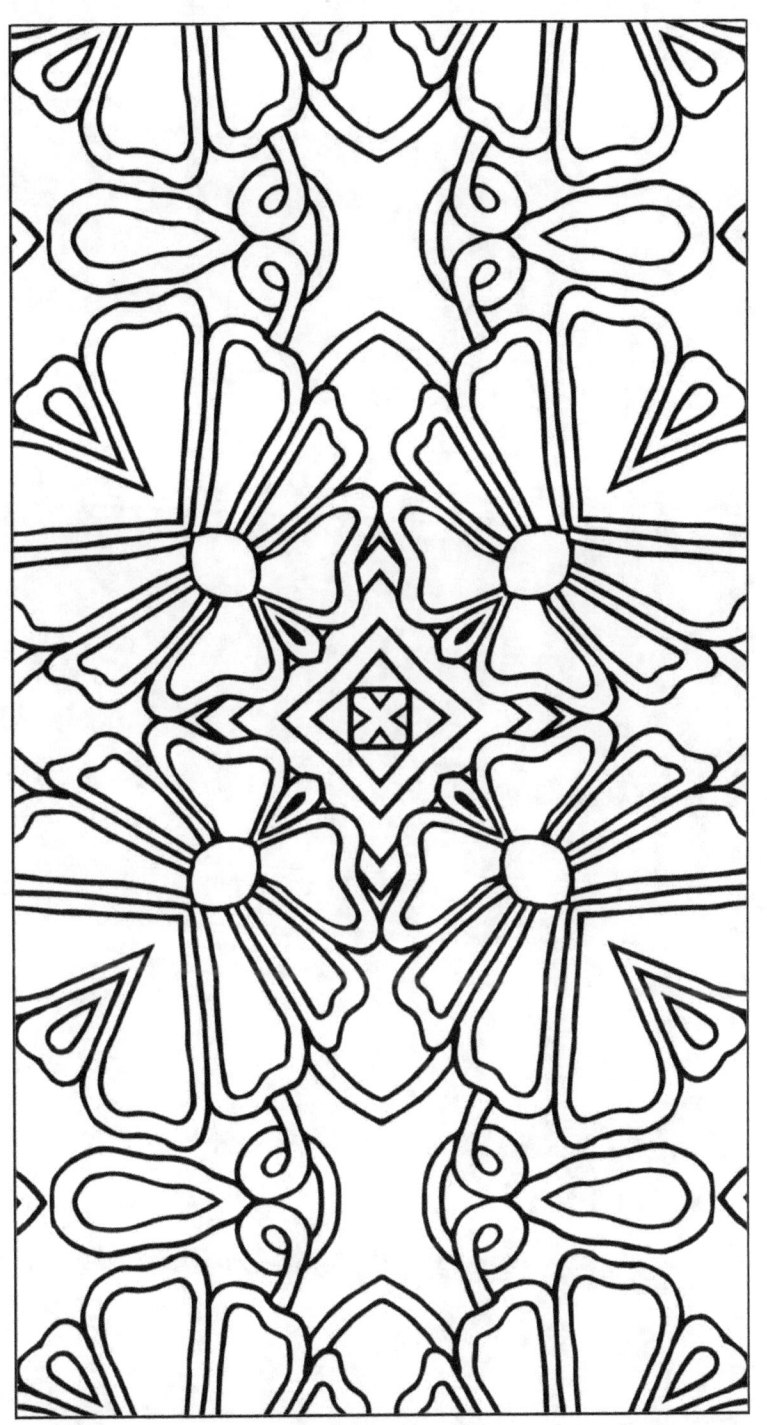

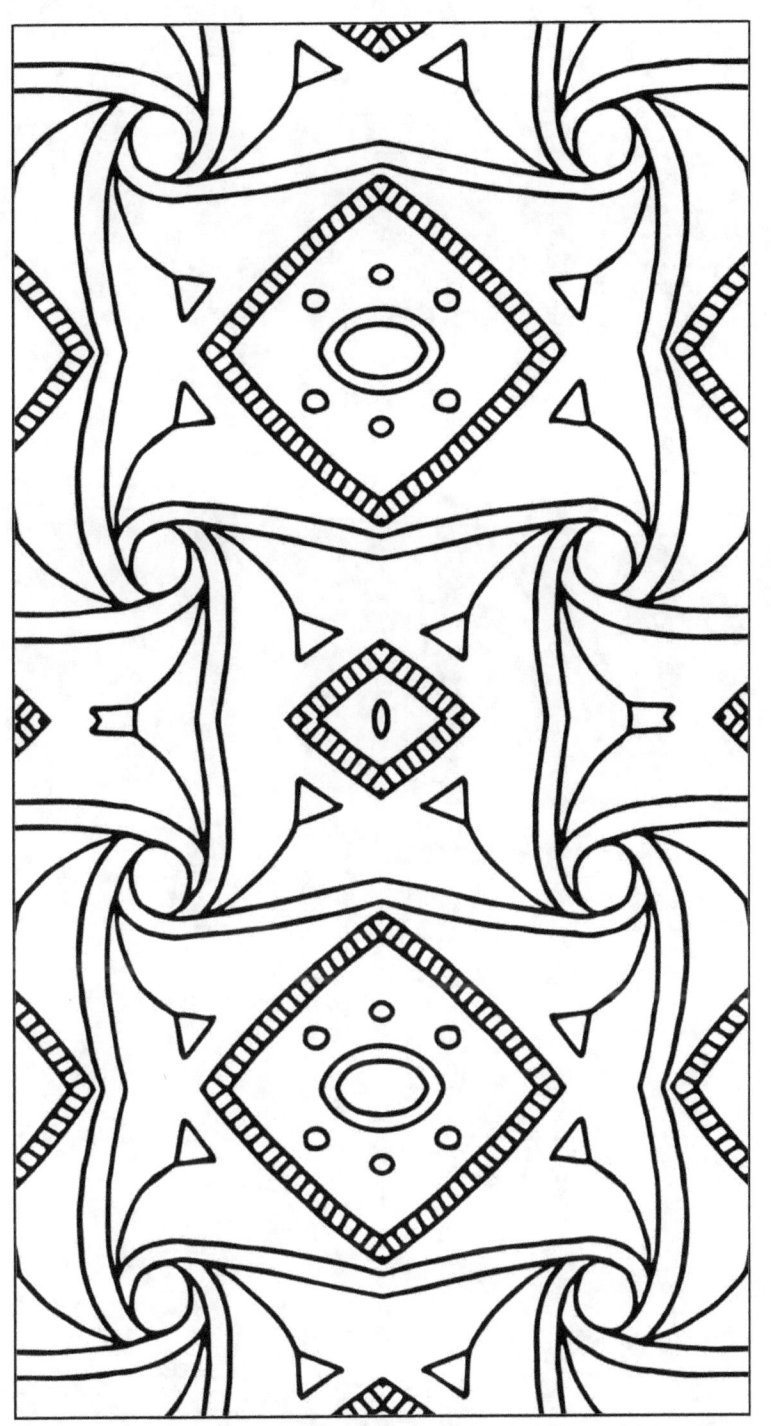

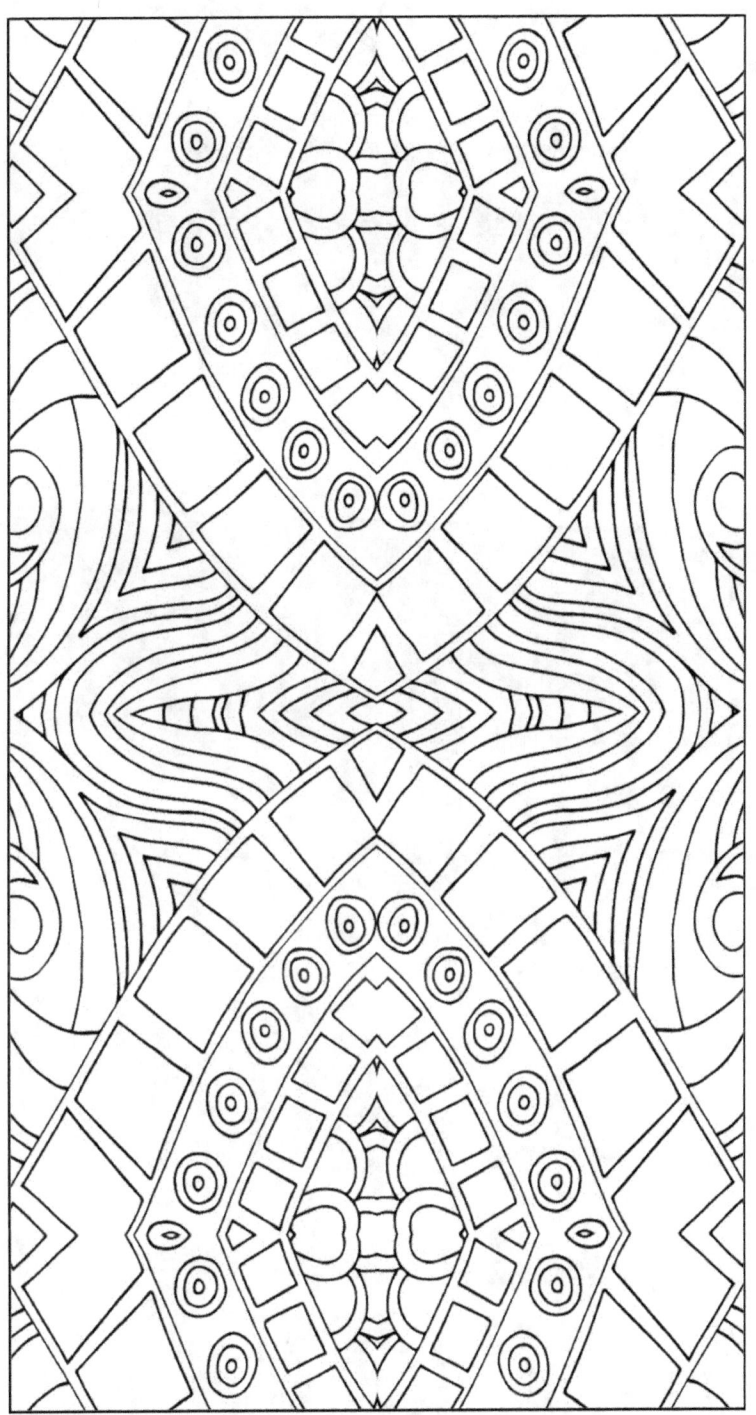

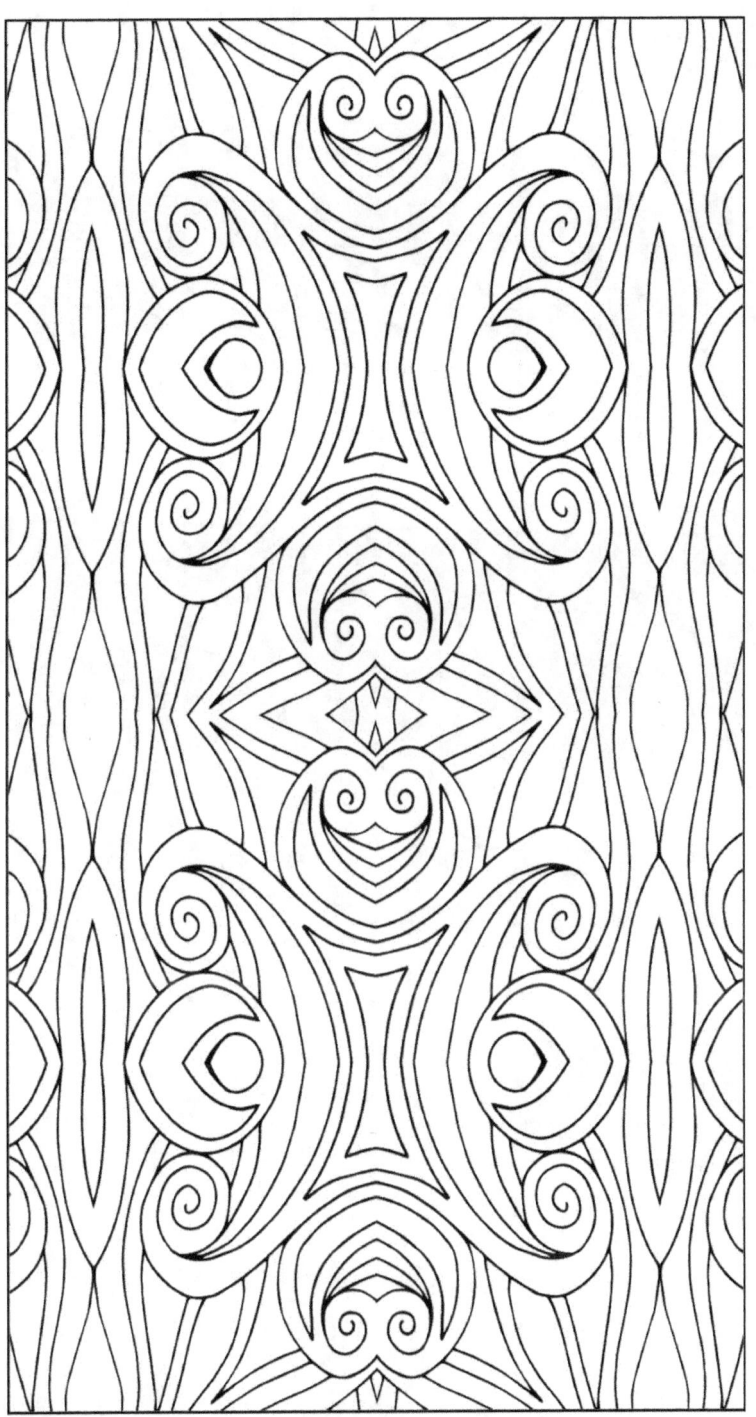

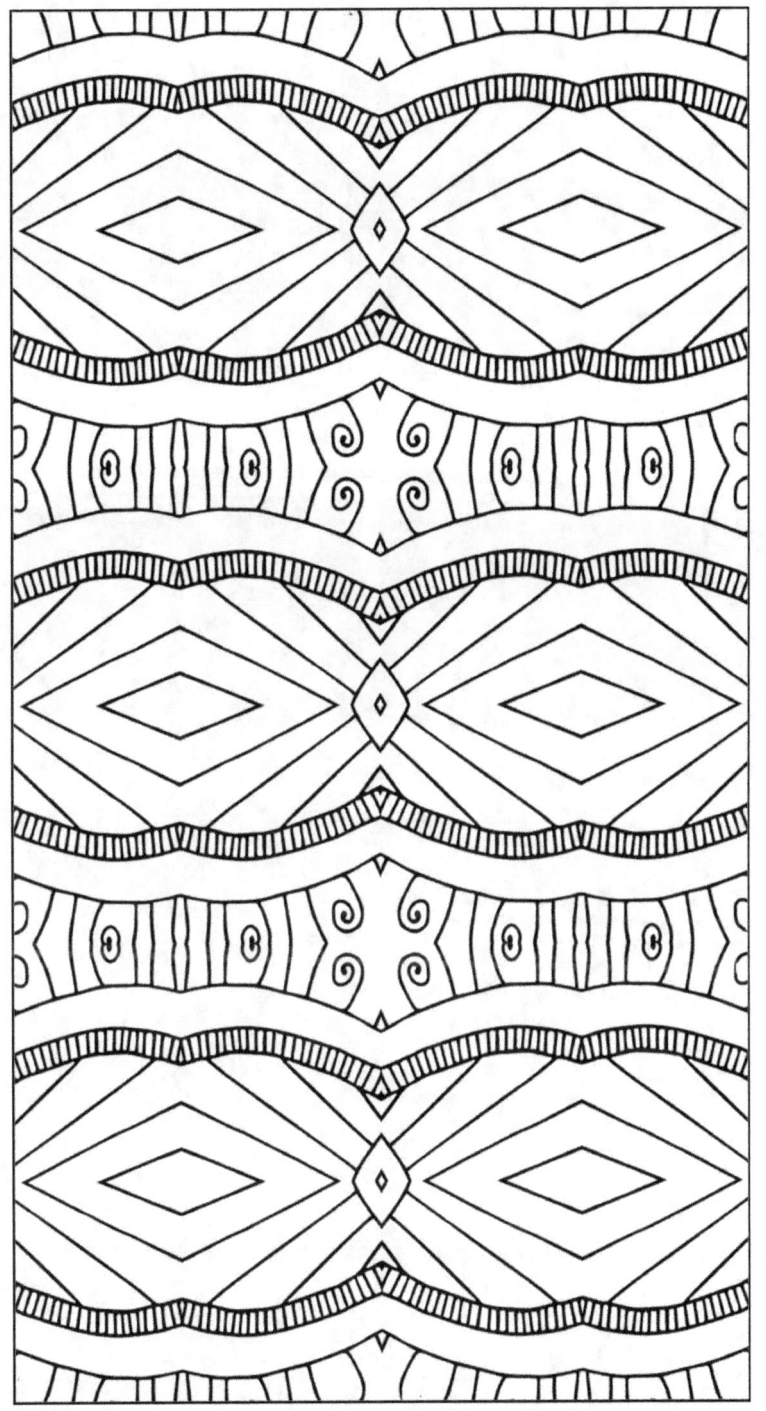

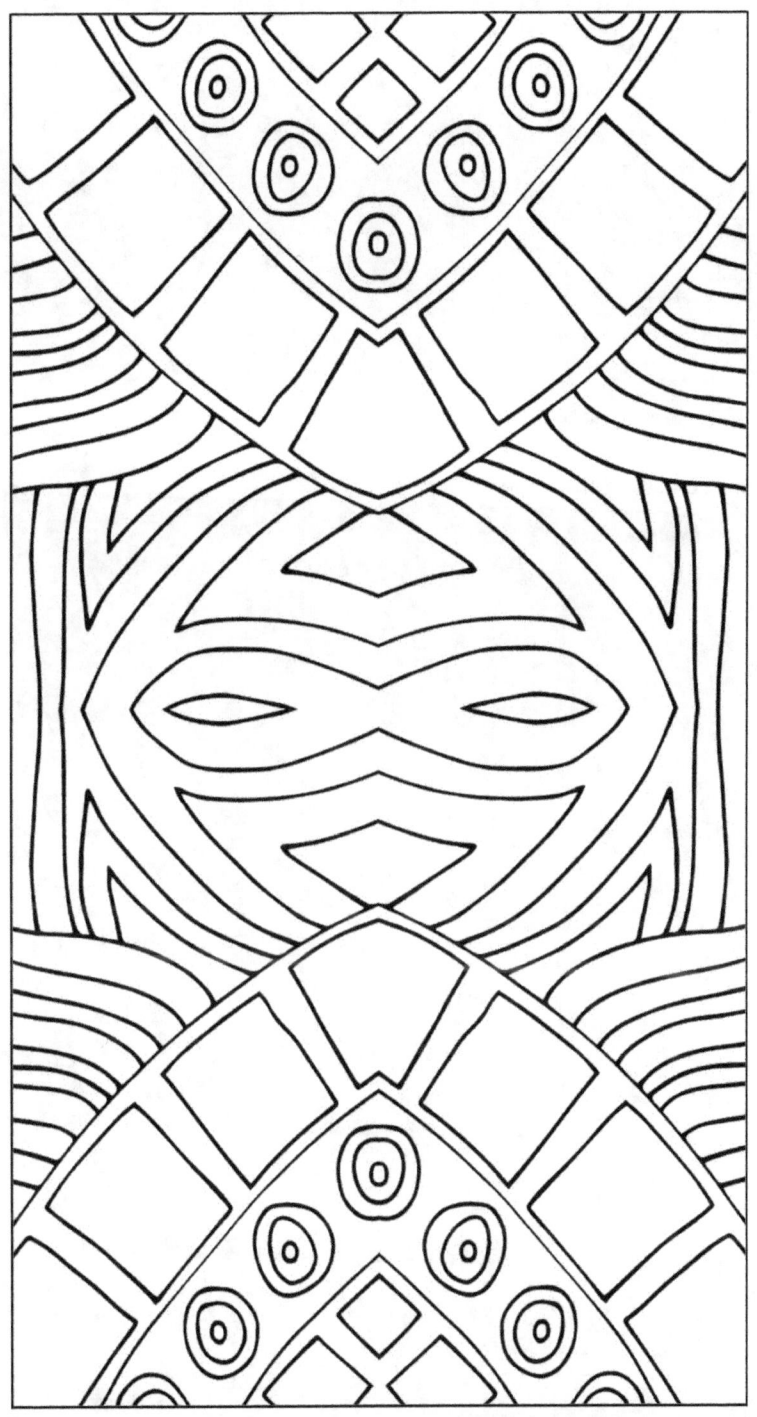

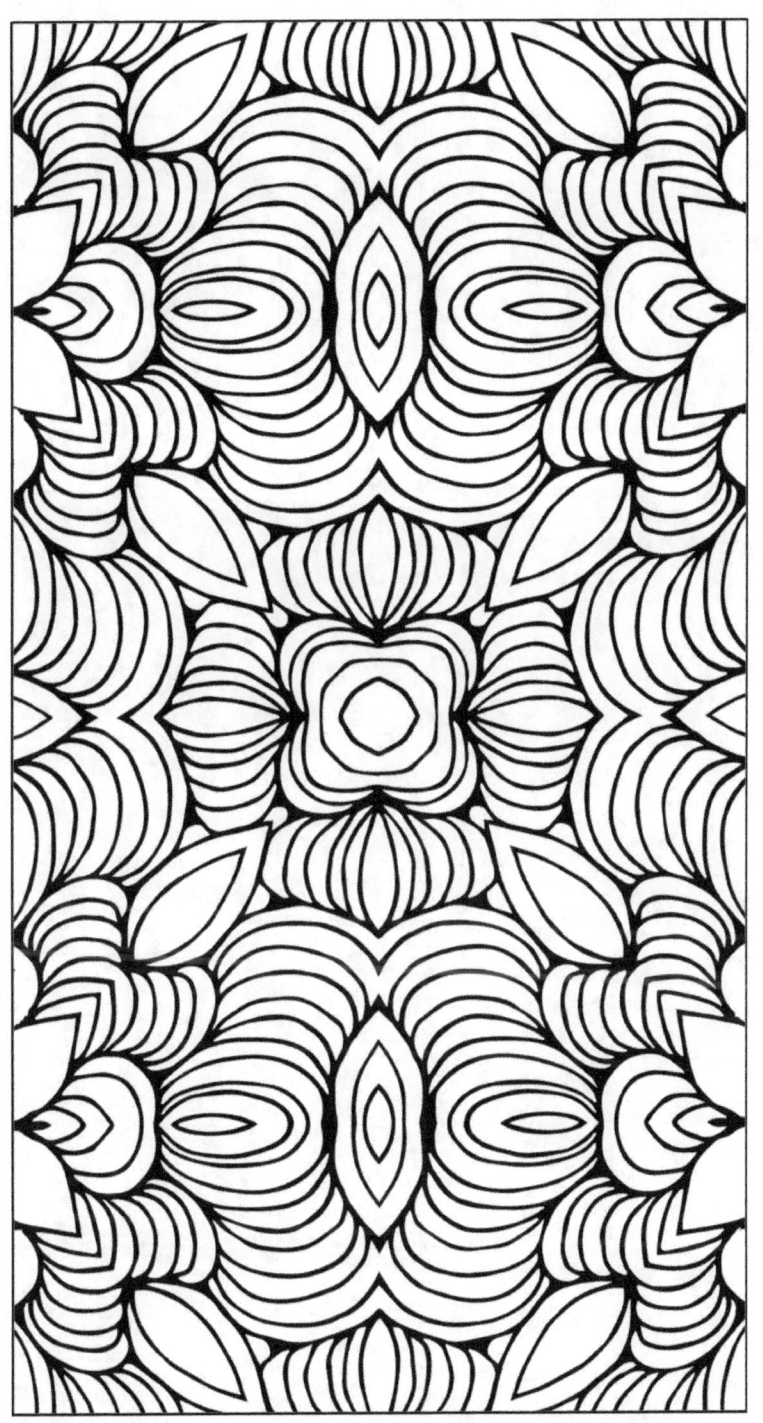

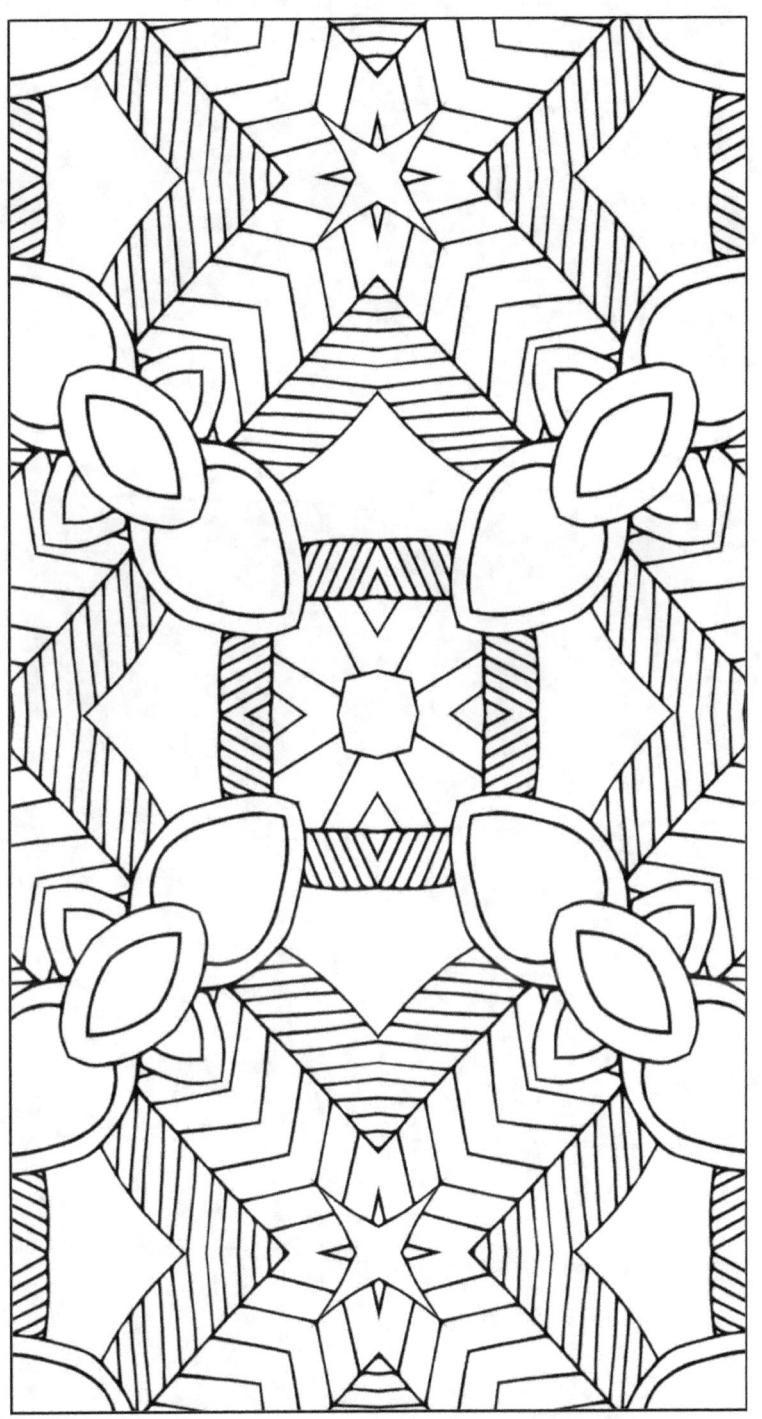

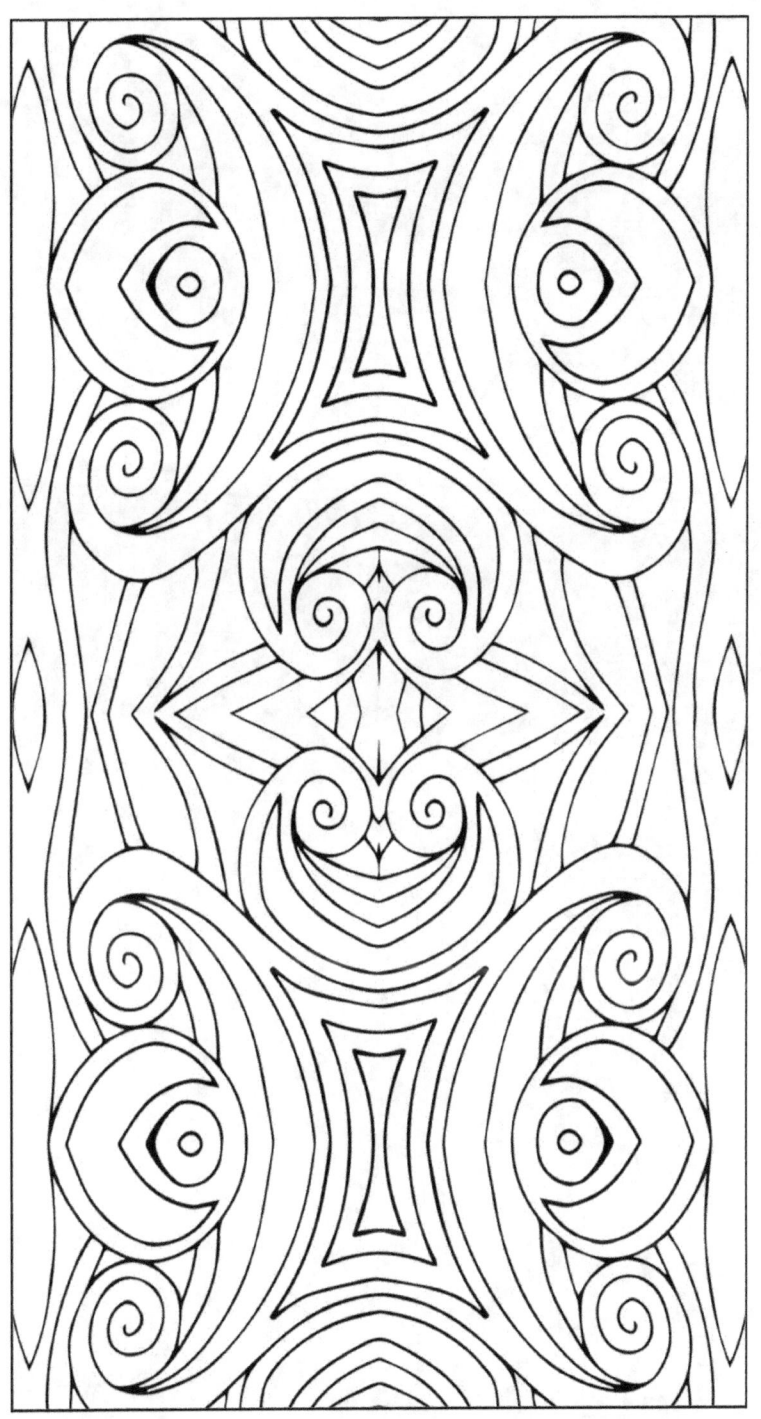

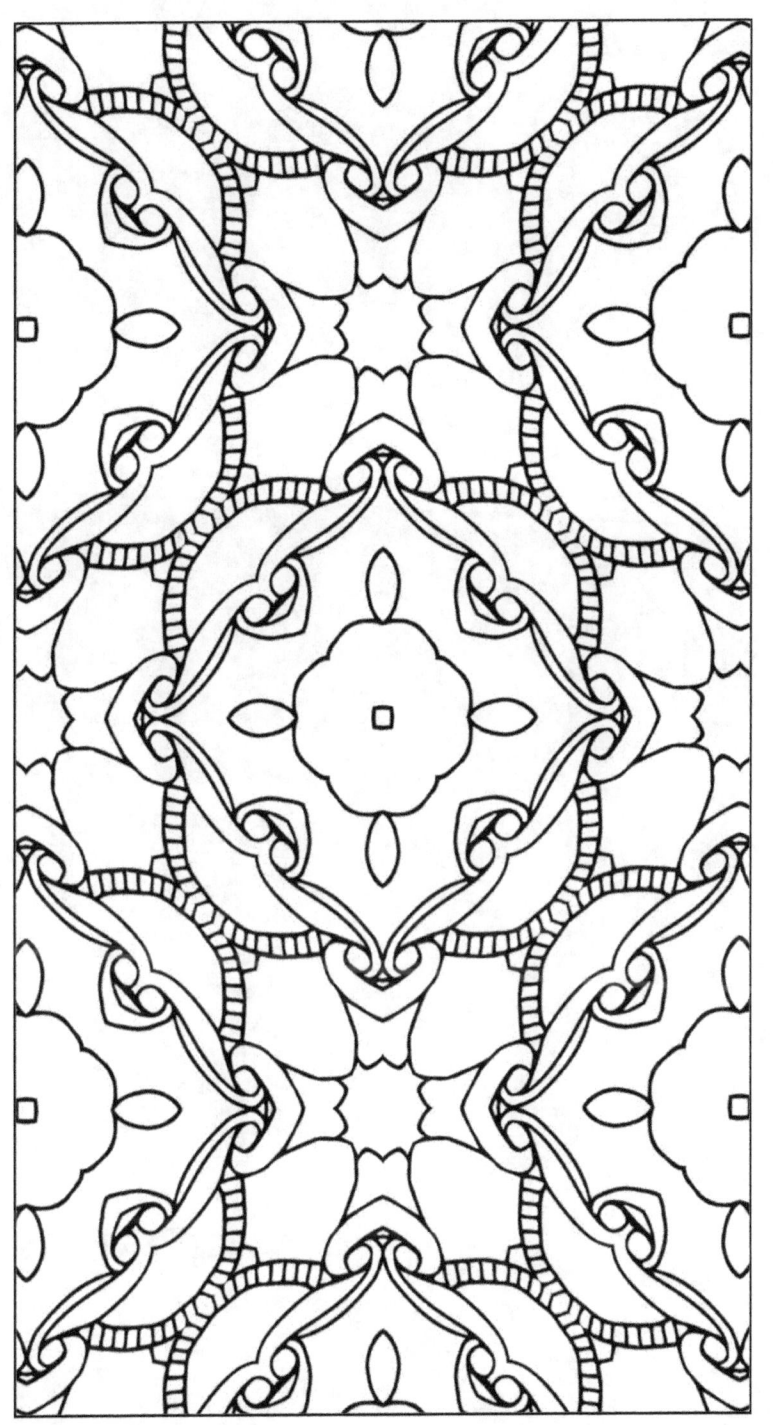

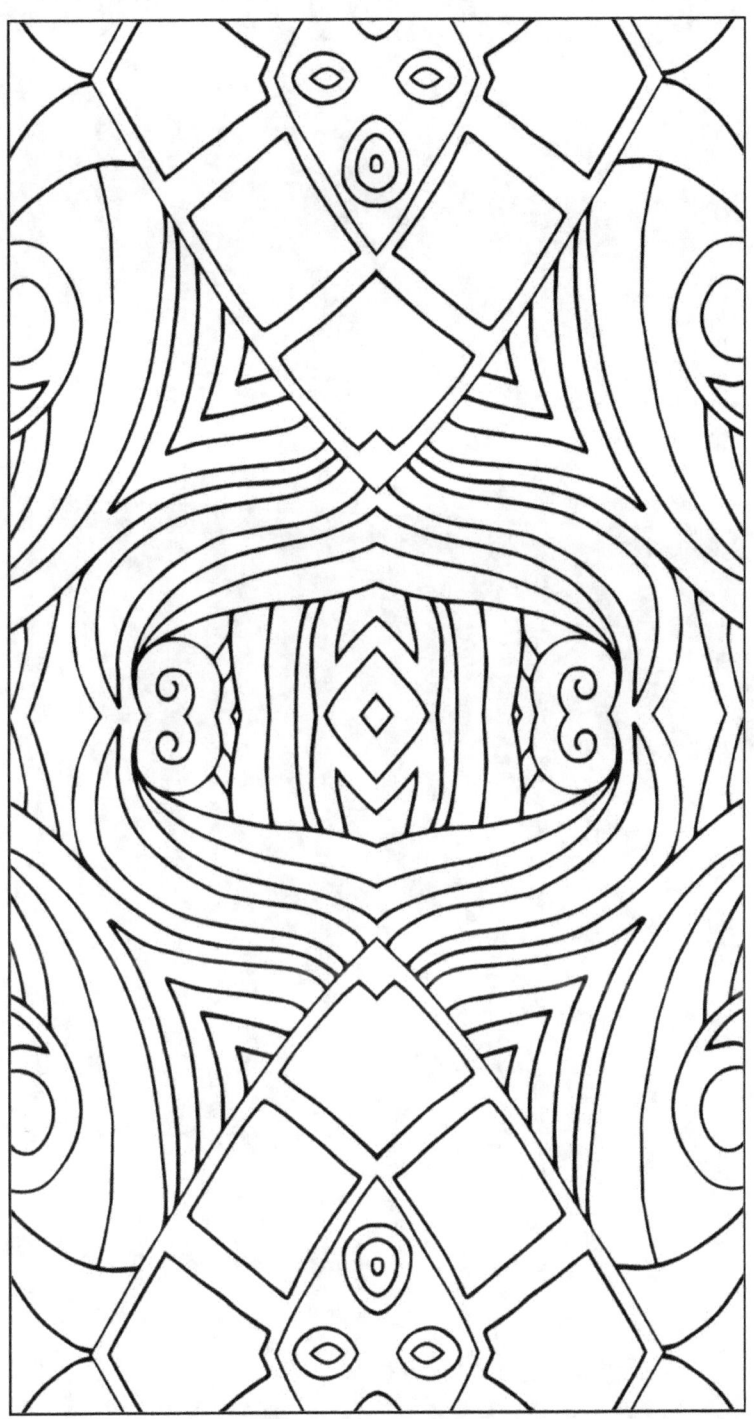

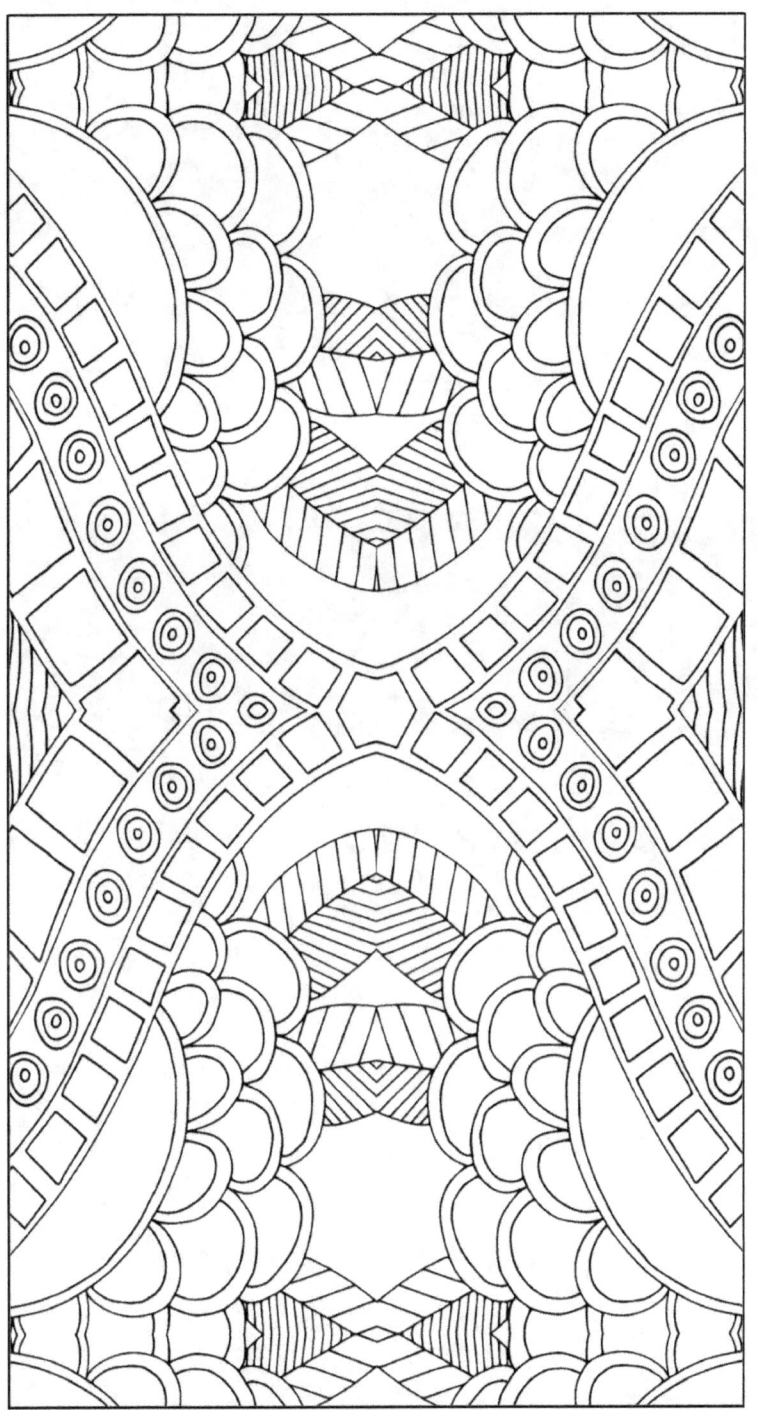

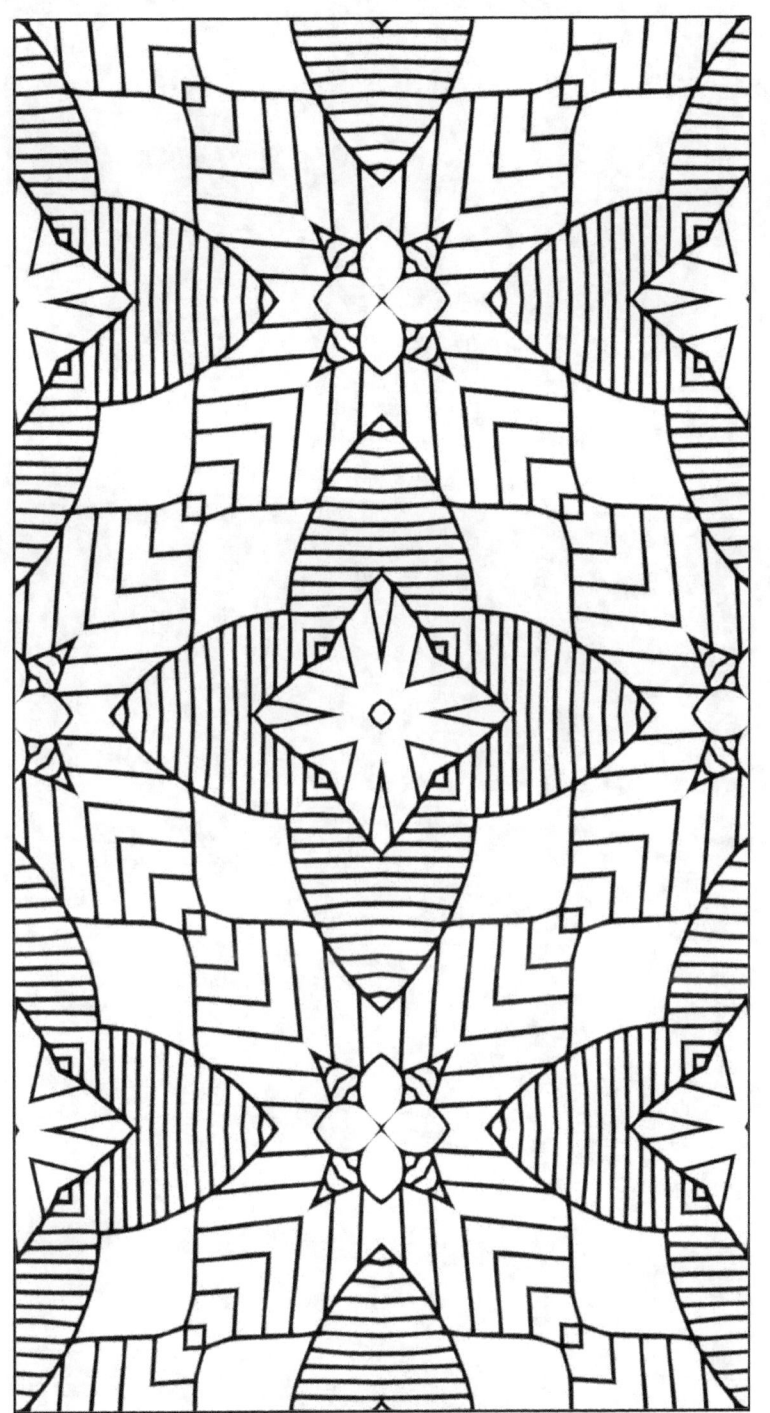

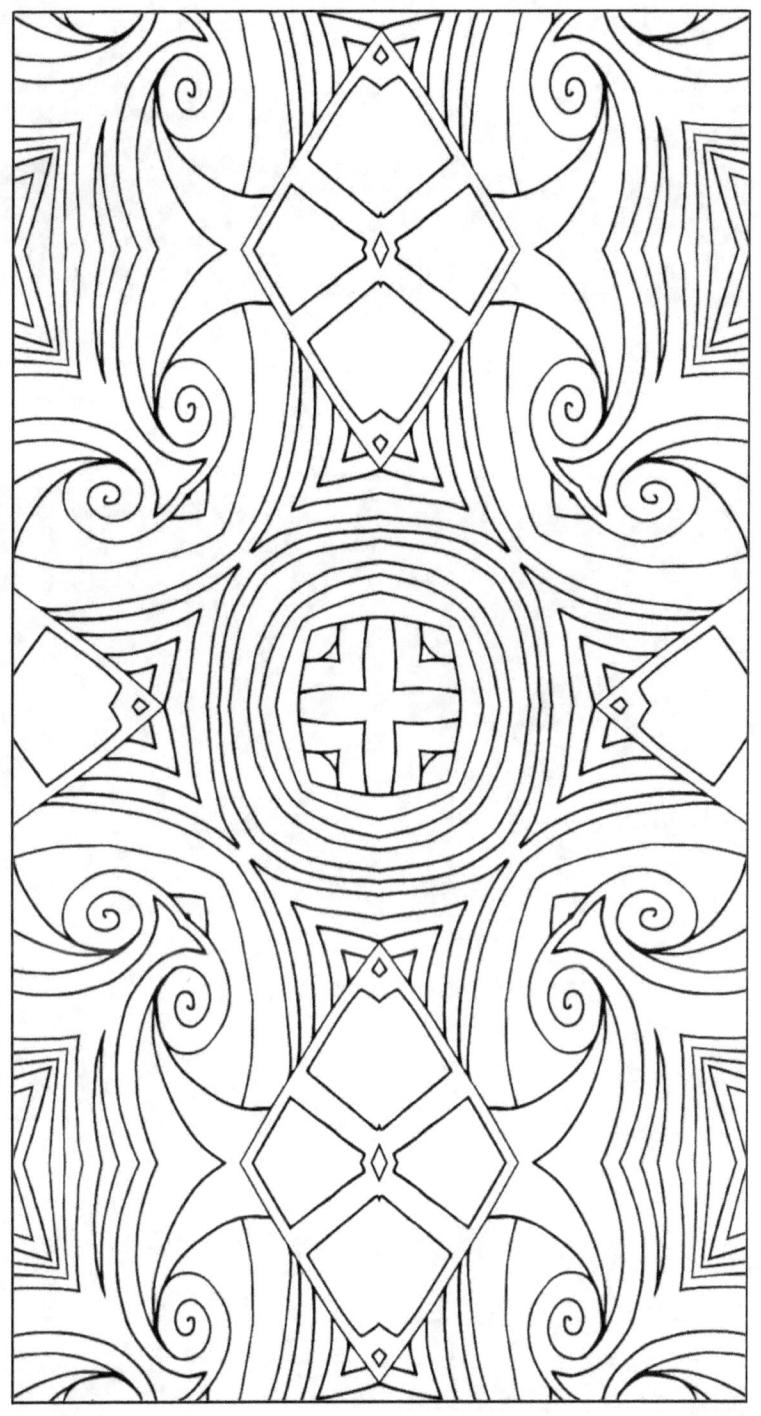

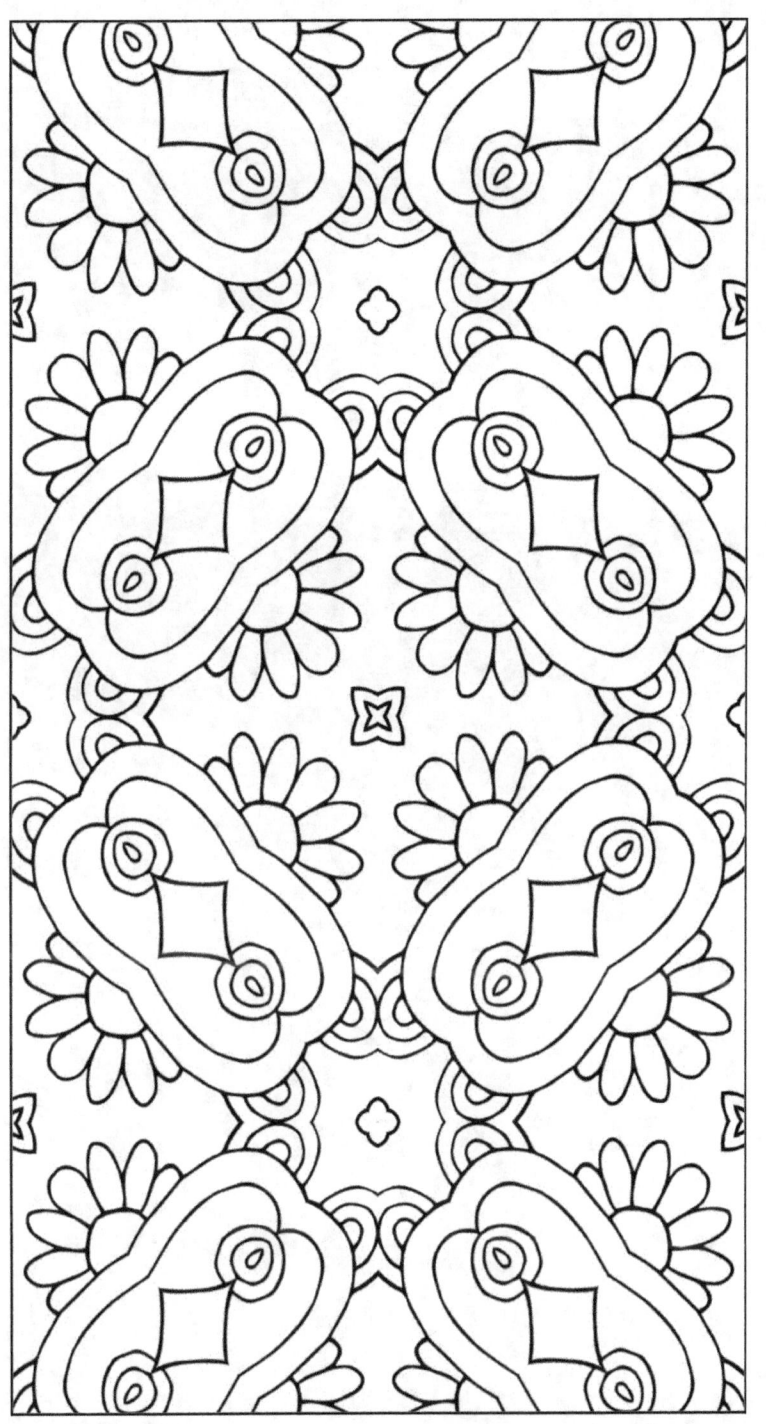

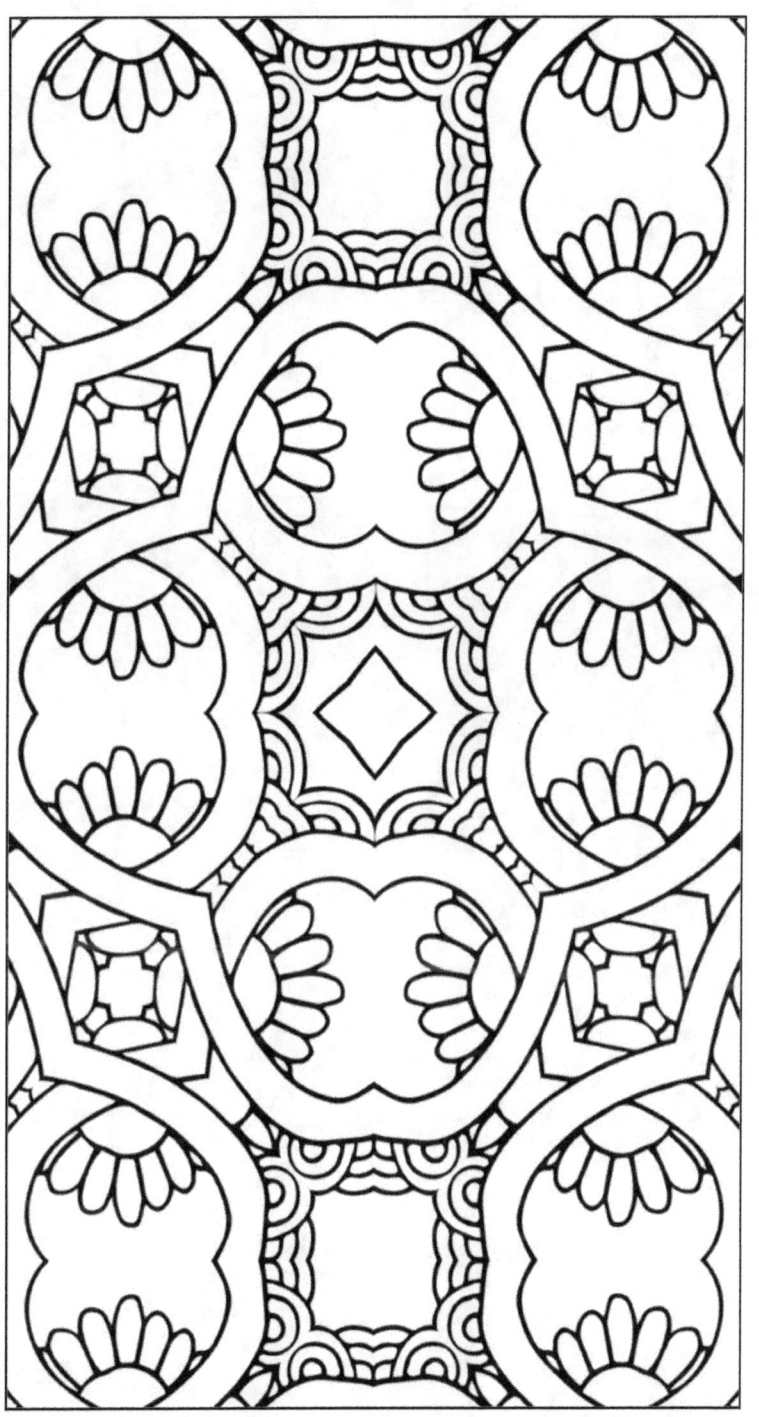

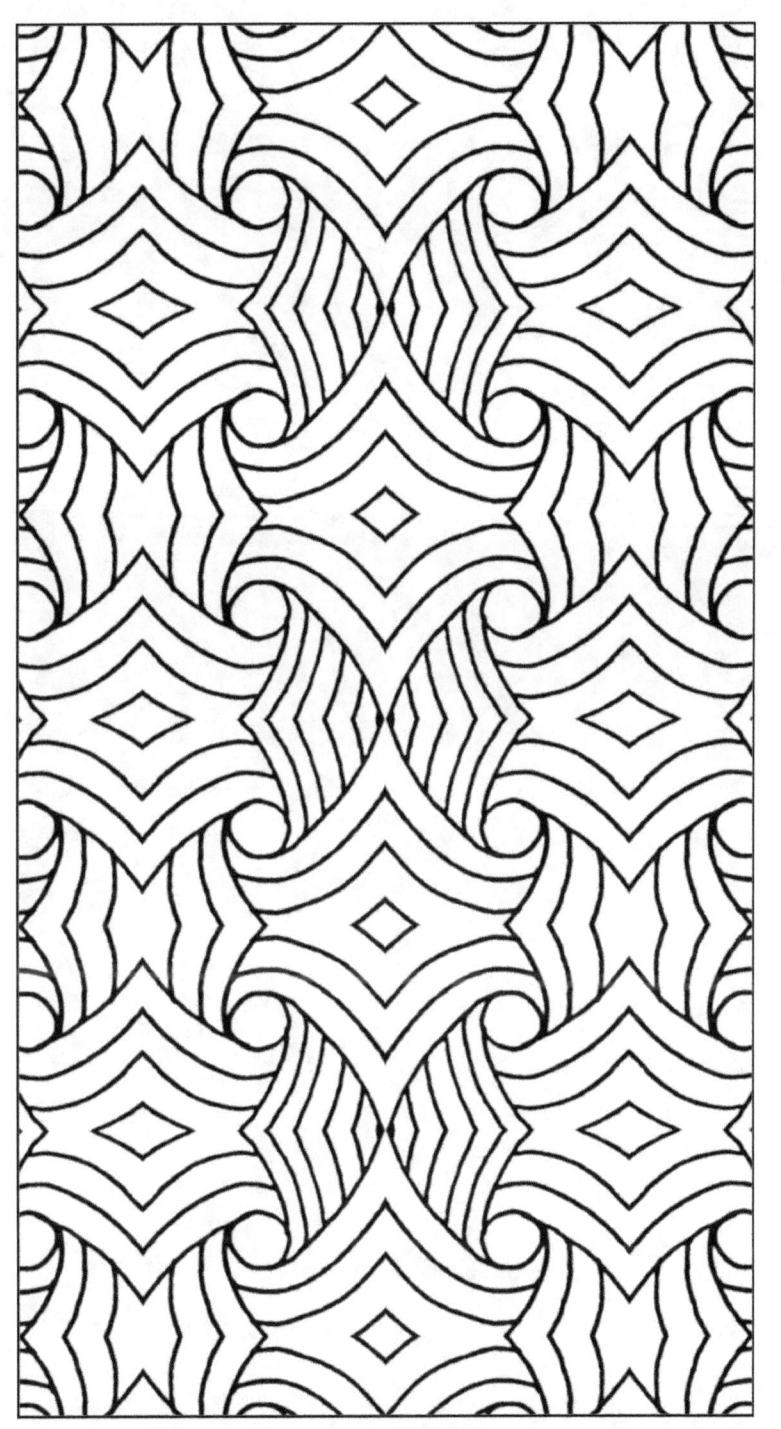

Blank Page

Remove and Insert Between
Pages if Using Wet Media

Blank Page

Remove and Insert Between
Pages if Using Wet Media

www.ingramcontent.com/pod-product-compliance
Lightning Source LLC
Chambersburg PA
CBHW070431180526
45158CB00017B/967